NOW
MAKE
GOOD

CHAS WILSON

Now Make Good

Copyright © 2017 Chas Wilson

Published by Master Networks Publishing
www.MasterNetworksPublishing.com

ISBN: 978-1-943157-41-9

Printed in the United States of America

For more information or to reach the author, go to:

www.ChasWilson.com

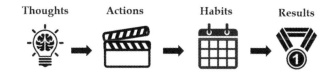

Thoughts   Actions   Habits   Results

PREFACE

Does the word *promise* mean something? Or is it just a word? Try telling your kids that you promise to do something and then *not* do it! "But, Dad, you promised!" Apparently, I have promised all kinds of things because my children use that line all the time. They are smart and know that the word *promise* means something.

We all start things we intend to complete, but then don't. We make goals that we know we won't hit. We tell our significant other a variety of things, or make promises to our kids, and then we don't follow through. Some of us can't say "No," and so by saying "Yes" to everything, we are essentially saying "No" to something else. The resulting impact then becomes a label that we carry. We become known as someone who can't be counted on. And that's not good!

I was reading an in-flight magazine on the flight back from a speaking engagement and came across the story of Alex Sheen. On the morning of September 4, 2012, Alex's father passed away of small-cell lung cancer. Alex was asked to speak at his father's funeral. During the eulogy he chose to speak about the way his father kept his promises. "Too often we say things like, 'I will get to it tomorrow' and guess what, one day there isn't tomorrow," he said. The promises and commitments we make really do mean something. They define us.

Alex's speech was entitled "Because I said I would." It was on that day that, for the first time, he handed out what he called

"Promise Cards" to serve as simple reminders of keeping people's commitments.

You simply write a promise on the card and then give it to the person to whom you are making the promise. Or you can take a picture and post it on social media. Alex Sheen started a social movement on his site: http://www.becauseisaidiwould.com. To date, Alex and his team have distributed over 5.46 million promise cards to over 153 different countries.

How do you keep commitments? How are you showing up? What legacy are you leaving? We are each building a legacy for those who come behind us.

That's what this book is all about. I initially started this book for the selfish purpose of providing a training resource for the leaders of my organizations. I quickly realized through my research how applicable this is for so many others. My goal is to help each of us learn to live a purpose-driven life by design, to follow through on what we say we are going to do, and fulfill the goals that lead to success. Together we can!

TABLE OF CONTENTS

FOREWORD

Back in the fall of 1997, I had just finished up my first year of college and consequently, my first time living away from home. This newfound freedom had allowed me some time to reflect on not just what I wanted to *do* when I grew up but also *who* I wanted to be when I grew up. It was during this time when I realized that I needed to serve and add value to other people in order to discover who I wanted to be. This required giving to others. I needed to serve this world before I took from the world. The result was a decision to do some church missionary service work.

I was first stationed in eastern Utah near the Colorado border. Part of this area covered some Indian reservations. After some time, I realized that my experiences were falling short of my expectations. In my naivety, I was taken by surprise at the lack of acceptance by many of the Native Americans on the reservations. Despite my willingness to serve and help them, sometimes they simply didn't want our help. It became frustrating.

The reality of being a fairly immature 19-20-year-old *far* away from home – trying to learn how to get along with other people with vastly different backgrounds and life experiences, finding myself placed in a position of leadership with immense responsibility that I had never before known – ended up being the recipe for a perfect storm. In the midst of all this was an overwhelming feeling of homesickness at being away from family, friends, and a girlfriend. Truth be told, I wanted to throw a pity party. And I did. A big one! These feelings of discouragement, frustration, inadequacy, and homesickness continued for a few weeks.

Every month we met with the leader of our mission service to give updates and report on progress and activities. It was a time for everyone to receive additional training and support.

Hugh Gregson stood about 6'5," weighed around 250 pounds, and had size 15 shoes. We all became very familiar with his physical stature – as he often reminded us when we dared to step out of line. He was an intimidating man but had a servant's heart and was a great leader.

One day, I was called into his office to give my update and report the progress of our assistance. I expressed my homesickness and proceeded to question whether or not I wanted to continue in the program. I sought for his advice. I don't know if I expected pity from him or understanding and acceptance for how I felt, but I wasn't getting any of that. As I expressed my frustrations, he sat across from the desk with his legs and arms crossed. His eyes were focused directly on me. They were piercing.

He leaned over the desk and said very boldly, "I will give you some advice that I want you to burn into your heart and mind for the rest of your life. You signed up as a tough guy, now make good." What he meant was this: *You signed up for this – no one forced you to be here. You came on your own free will. You volunteered to give of your time, effort, and energy. You hired up as a tough guy, now make good. Burn that in your heart.*

I left that meeting a different person! I now separated my expectation from my experience. And my experiences no longer defined my failed expectations. The next few days I spent in meditation, reflection, and prayer as Hugh's words continued to roll through my mind. I would hear them over and over again. I tried every way I could to rationalize why it would be okay to quit.

But he was entirely correct. I had volunteered and made a commitment, a *promise* to myself and others. I knew that this feeling of frustration would be temporary and that I would regret it later on if I did not follow through on my commitment. I knew that if I could learn this, it would benefit me for the rest of my life…and it has.

Over the past 20 years of my life, I have realized that there are some things tough guys do when they step up. This book will highlight those characteristics and actions that help us be tough – of being commitment-makers and promise-keepers. At the time of writing this book, I can say that these principles have helped me have a successful marriage, an amazing relationship with my five children, and lead the more than 30 companies I own.

This is an amazing time in our history. With the introduction of cell phones and social media, everything is being documented. Something you do today could (and probably will) be seen by your children or grandchildren in 20 years! It's incredible to think that so much of what we do is being captured and recorded.

What story are you telling? What is left untold? What kind of legacy are you building? You only get one shot at this… Live Big!

This book is meant to challenge you to define the legacy you are leaving. Be bold! Act now! Follow through on the things you have committed to and promised!

Eleanor Roosevelt has been credited with saying "Yesterday is history, tomorrow is a mystery, and today is a gift; that's why they call it the present."

The only time you have is now! It is time to…NOW MAKE GOOD!

INTRODUCTION

For those who want more, for those who want to make a difference, for those who are committed to success, this book is for you!

So what is success? The good news is that each of us define our own success! But make no mistake – you must define it. Unless you define what success is for you, how will you know if you are making progress or if you have achieved success? I believe that I have a moral duty to be successful! Not just for me, but for those who count on me! I have a moral and ethical obligation to those who love me, for those I love, and for those who will come into my life in the future to be successful.

The challenge for most of us is how to achieve the desired results that leads to success.

Consider the following diagram:

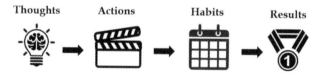

Thoughts lead to actions, actions lead to creating habits, and habits lead to results! These are the steps to achieving the success results that we desire. It all starts with our thoughts, not our actions. Really think about that! Any time I want to create a different result in my life, the most natural first step is to take action, but it actually starts with changing my thinking.

Once I have my thinking right, then I get into action! Once I determine my actions are leading me toward the results I desire, I work to develop that action into a habit. This process is what will lead you to the results you desire.

If you want to get that next promotion, if you want to get that higher paying job, if you want to develop longer lasting relationships, if you want to get in better shape, or whatever it is that you want to improve or achieve, you can implement this process for each area of your life that you are looking to improve.

> Life is a journey ... but it is also about results.

As you move into mastery of this process, you will see an increase in success in your life. You will discover that more is possible and, most importantly, that it is achievable!

Yes, life is a journey. But, life is also about the destination – the results! Think about it…you don't take a flight simply to fly. You take a flight to get to your destination!

Consider the football team that makes it to the championship game only to lose the game. They may tell themselves, "Team, I know we lost but we had a great season anyway." Making statements like these only deflect from the truth that they lost. All the hard work is for the result of winning the championship. Don't lose sight that results do matter! Don't let others, especially those who are not living up to their potential, tell you that results do not matter. Achieving the success that you define matters!

It is time to dream again! It is time to think big again! It is time to make good on all the promises you've made to yourself and others! It is time to…NOW MAKE GOOD!

CHAPTER ONE

THOUGHTS

THOUGHTS

—THE LEARNING MINDSET

Nothing good happens by accident. I must make it happen. If it's meant to be, then it is up to me! I assume control of the way I think and how I think. This drives me into activity.

Everything we do begins with our thinking and our thoughts – our mindset. It's all in the *way* we think and *how* we think, not just *what* we think. Are we open to learning new things that challenge our mindset?

The power of the mind is truly incredible. A single thought can lead us to do amazing things. Yet so many of us lack discipline when it comes to controlling what we think and the way in which we think.

Author and political theorist Benjamin Barber described mindset by stating, "I don't divide the world into the weak and the strong, or the successes and the failures, or those who make it or those who don't. I divide the world into learners and non-learners."

From an early age, I would often get frustrated with not knowing why I needed to do something. When my teachers asked us to color on a page, read a specific story, or do a certain activity, I seemed to always ask, "Why? Why are we doing this? Why should we read this?"

Thoughts

I wasn't asking the question to cause trouble or be

defiant. I simply wanted to know why and how that activity benefited me. I figured there must be some important reason I needed to do what I had been told, and I only wanted to know why.

This process of questioning allows me to understand the "why" behind any task, goal, or objective. The truth is that once I understand the "why," I can focus on how to accomplish the goal, task, or objective. Asking questions is a vital thinking skill that one must learn to be able to truly buy-in to the goals ahead. If you are not able to fully "buy-in," then you should start by asking more questions.

I have empowered those who are closest to me to challenge me when they notice my thinking isn't congruent with my goals. I want them to hold me to a higher standard of thinking and help me eliminate entertaining the ominous thoughts of "can't," "won't," "impossible," or "unachievable."

Henry Ford has been attributed with saying, "Whether you think you can, or you think you can't – you're right."

If that is true, and I believe it is, then isn't it incredibly important to focus on our mindset? If we know that the entire key to progress and improvement starts with our thought process, then it is vital to improve our mindset.

By taking the time to imagine, invent, and plan, we will find ways to improve, enhance, and expand. The more we improve upon our thinking and mindset, then the more control we will have in our own positive progression and the more positive influence we will exert upon others around us. When we master the ability to control our thoughts and our way of thinking, we become the architects of, and take control of, our own personal destiny.

Thoughts

How do we control our thoughts and our way of thinking? How do we improve our destiny? The steps to helping me improve my thoughts are: having a clear vision, a purposeful "why," positive self-talk, and controlling my environment. Unless I focus on these steps to improve my thinking, I cannot progress toward the desired results.

Vision

Some people end up changing the world. Henry Ford, Thomas Edison, Sam Walton, and Steve Jobs are among the many who have. They created products and services that weren't around before they created them. More importantly, they create things, services, ideas, and a future that others only dreamed about. They started with a vision, they took action, and made it happen.

> Where there is vision, the people will prosper.

Therefore, we don't call them "dreamers" (the world has enough of those); instead, we call them "visionaries." They think, they see, they act, they create – and that is a far cry from just dreaming. Before anything is acted upon or created, we must first have a dream or vision for what is possible and then have the courage to take the necessary path to make it happen.

You may have heard the great proverb, "Where there is no vision, the people will perish." The opposite is also true. Where there is a vision, the people will prosper! Take time to create and craft a vision statement for yourself, your business, your family, and your future. Committing time and energy to create a statement is a very powerful act. These statements tell those around you what you are doing and where you are heading. Once you

Thoughts create these statements, then you have a mental framework for the foundation of the vision.

Moreover, one immediate benefit of crafting such a statement is that once in place, those around you have a sense of how best to support you on your path.

No one else can really write this statement for you, although others can help improve upon the words or clean it up. The power of the vision statement comes from the depths of the most center part of your heart and is a reflection of how much you believe in the words as they are written. Placing these thoughts and feelings into actual words is a way of giving them a sense of reality. This is why your vision statement must come from you.

Strong Sense of Your "Why"

Your *why* is what drives you. It is what gets you out of bed each day and pushes you through each grueling challenge. Some say it should be powerful enough to make you cry. Your *why* is not *what* you do – your *why* is the *reason* you do what you do.

Any person, company, or organization can share *what* it does. Some are even experts at how they do what they do. They are experts of their technical skill or gift. But most are unable to explain *why* they do what they do.

So many of us self-identify with "what" we do. For example, if I asked you what you do, you might reply, "chiropractor," or "insurance agent," or "realtor," or some other occupation. We have become so conditioned with this response, it becomes easy to forget *why* we do what we do. What if instead of saying, "I am a chiropractor," your response was that you help people who are in pain become pain-free? Replying in this manner takes away the label, and places an emphasis on *why* you are a chiropractor.

Thoughts

My personal *why* has changed several times

throughout the course of my career. As I have become clear on my *why*, I can then be more committed to my *what*.

My *why* is actually very important to me and because of its personal nature I don't share it with many people. In fact, I might even say that my *why* is sacred to me. Without going into the specifics of my *why*, I will share that it has to do with my wife and children.

For many years I had a 3x5 postcard with the following quote: "Are you married to this?" This was to help remind me, as it got late in the day, that I was not married to the work (the *what*) and if I wanted to stay married to my wife (my *why*), then I had better remember my *why* and get home! The act of setting the priority of when I would be home aided in developing the necessary balance to our home and relationship.

If you can't clearly describe your why, then take some time to think about what is important to you and why you do what you do. Getting clear on your *why* will help you develop the desire to think beyond yourself.

I recently spoke with someone who shared that his *why* was about building a legacy that reached for generations. I could feel his energy, conviction, and passion behind his *why*! Your *why* should be established with the same conviction and passion.

Planning

Once your vision becomes clear and is powered with a strong *why*, the next step is to create the plan that will form your path. It's not enough to know what you are reaching for, but **Thoughts** vital to know which steps to take to reach that destination. In my experience consulting business owners, I have found that most people spend more time planning a week-long vacation than they do in planning their futures.

In athletic competitions, the team with the best game plan usually wins. With regard to entrepreneurs, the best business plan will more than likely achieve success at the highest possible level.

The easiest plans to understand are simple and can be reduced to a single page. I like to use the 1-3-5 GPS Planning System. It's like a GPS guidance system because it gets you to where you want to go.

> 1 – Goal (your goal)
> 3 – Priorities (help you reach your goal)
> 5 – Steps (steps to reach your priority)

This guide can be used to approach any challenge, unlock any opportunity, and is a way to begin with the end in mind. It works well for a one-hour meeting, a business planning session, organizational planning, or a family plan.

Whether it's used as a tool to determine the way to increase sales, membership, or a family reunion, the GPS helps.

However, it is more than a system. It's a way to think, providing foresight and insight. It helps you take action! It unlocks creativity, and creates clarity and focus. It is a proven and effective tool for anyone who has a strong vision yet needs to define the pathway for reaching their goals.

1 – Goal

It is incredibly important that you shoot for one goal. Most likely you will have several goals in your head, but narrowing these to the most important goal is the key. Keep the goal specific and measurable so that you will know if you are on track. In *The One Thing*, authors Gary

Thoughts

Keller and Jay Papasan phrase it this way: "What's the ONE thing I can do such that by doing it everything else will be easier or unnecessary?"

What a wonderful question to lead you to push yourself higher each and every time you ask it! I ask this question each time I think I have settled on a goal: will accomplishing that goal make everything else easier or unnecessary?

3 – Priorities
This step is to clarify the strategies or sets of actions that will most likely lead to the accomplishment of the goal.

Make a list of the action-oriented priorities that you believe will be most effective in accomplishing the goal. The key factor is this: *What can I **do** to accomplish my goal?*

5 – Steps
This part is where you clarify the specific things you can do to make each of your three outlined priorities come to pass. While the minimum number of steps isn't as important, make sure you have no more than five.

> Don't say it if you don't mean it.

The 1-3-5 GPS Planning System is a thought process that takes time, focus, and effort. It also requires an ability to make decisions and to analytically think through each step.

At first this process may seem cumbersome, but like any new skill, it takes time to learn. I assure you that it will get easier with practice. The end results are worth the effort because they are built upon the foundation of a clear vision powered by a strong *why.*

Thoughts

Self-Talk

It's great to utilize a vision statement and a plan as a path toward accomplishment of a goal. But there is one tool that can be most helpful in keeping us on track: *self-talk*. This is the conversation we have in our own heads. It's that inner voice we hear when we really pay attention. Our minds have such enormous power, for both good and bad. If we are not careful, we can easily allow negative talk to seep into our minds.

In fact, most people are so accustomed to the negative talk that they are not aware of just how easily it has crept into their everyday thinking. The first step is an awareness of the conversation. Then, you must change it into positive self-talk.

I am big fan of football, particularly college football. Every year, the Naval Academy football team posts a series of online videos documenting the season.

One recent video showed a former Naval Academy player, Clint Bruce, leading the team in a locker room motivational speech. He spoke about the team motto of "brotherhood." He said that this motto has stuck with him for years, and he knows that when he is with any other Naval Academy player, past or present, he is with his brothers.

In the video, Bruce asks the team to join him in the middle of the locker room for a rally breakdown. With hands raised in the middle, he says, "Brotherhood on three…and don't say it if you don't mean it!" That last phrase: "Don't say it if you don't mean it!" has stuck with me. Words mean something. Bruce's statement helped his team understand that their *why* went deeper than simply performing on the field. They were building a brotherhood.

Thoughts

The words you use – whether verbal or internal – are powerful. Here are some questions to reflect on your own self-talk: *How do you start your day? Do you immediately think about how excited you are for the day, or are you saying to yourself how you wish you could stay in bed?*

One of my mentors shared with me how he uses self-talk every day. Each morning as he stands in front of the mirror and shaves, he puts on aftershave, slaps his cheeks and says, "You handsome brute, don't you ever die!" I could only imagine what would happen if I stood in front of the mirror, slapped my cheeks, and said that. I am sure that I would get some sort of mocking, comment, or eye roll (or all of the above) from my wife. This would not be because she means to put me down or discourage me, but because she, like most of us, has been so conditioned to think that behavior like that might seem arrogant or cocky.

Even without intending to do so, some of the people around us may put us down or create a limiting belief in us. That's why we need to be positive about our own self-talk. The world is going to beat you up enough as it is. Don't join in. Controlling your own self-talk is a vital key to, and one of the first principles of, a successful mindset.

Create Your Environment

Notice the use of the word "create" when describing environment in the title above. I don't subscribe to the notion that I am a product of what happens to me, but rather what I create and do. Then, that being true, I can create the environment to support the desired mindset.

Thoughts Let me explain some of the best practices for creating environment as a support for fostering a positive mindset.

First, I make careful choices about what I listen to. The voices that I allow to be heard have a huge impact on my mindset and self-talk. If you hear something enough times, you start to believe it. This belief will create patterns in your life, and patterns become habits.

For me, each morning, a trip to the gym comes before going to the office, and this has developed into a routine habit. I prefer fast-paced music because it helps increase my energy early in the morning while I work out. One day the internet at the gym was not working and I was unable to stream the music to which I typically listen. The only things downloaded on my phone that didn't require the internet were some business audio books. So I opened a book and began listening.

> True friends tell you what you don't want to hear.

Fortunately, the book I picked was read by the actual author and his passion for the message was very enthusiastic. This made it easy to stay tuned in to the message. In fact, I was so engaged in the message that I got lost in my workout and spent far longer on the bike than normal. I realized that because my mind was so occupied with the content of this book, I wasn't feeling the fatigue I usually felt at this point. Or, was it that I just wasn't thinking about it?

The point that I am making here is that what you listen to will directly affect your routine, your habits, and your overall performance. You are a product of your environment.

Secondly, I purposefully choose encouraging relationships. It's important to understand that this is something I do with purpose and on purpose.

Thoughts

For a long time I wanted and kept friends who allowed me at times to complain, vent, or have a pity party with them. You know the phrase, "Misery loves company." Well, that was true with my friends. What I didn't understand is that true friends will tell me what I need to hear and not just what they think I want to hear. This makes all the difference.

Think about the people you spend the most time with. Do they challenge you to be better? Do they let you complain and then agree with you? Even worse, do they complain with you? Or, do they challenge you to push through the obstacles? Do they say the hard, right thing?

Once after a tough day at work, I walked through the door hoping to get my wife's ear and share my frustrations. As any perceptive partner and friend can do, she noticed the frustration before I even said a word.

As I walked over to her, she said, "What's going on? Is everything okay?"

I then began to share some of my complaints as she listened with focus and understanding. After a few minutes, she stood up and opened her arms to give me a hug. As we embraced, she whispered into my ear, "You hired up as a tough guy, now make good!"

My first reaction was, "Really?!... You're using my own motto against me!" But I quickly understood that she was right. A true partner and friend will tell you exactly what you need to hear and what you need to know.

You can, and need to be, purposeful about these relationships. The words and language they pour into you can shape your **Thoughts**   mindset, self-talk, and thinking. Choose wisely.

Belief and Commitment

Your commitments are directly connected to your beliefs. Have you ever started out really committed to getting in better shape? How long did you stay committed to that routine? Often, we lose our belief in our ability to accomplish the goal. When that happens, we tend to lose our commitment toward the goal.

In my businesses, I have a wide circle of regional leaders, partners, sales people, and even volunteers. I often find myself observing their level of commitment. Doing so offers clues about the level to which they believe in the mission we have developed as a team.

If I see the commitment of my members start to decrease, I know and understand that it is merely a symptom of their lack of belief. Instead of trying to make them feel guilty about the lack of commitment, we talk about their vision, their belief, and their *why*.

Culture

Mindset has everything to do with a culture. But first, we must ask: *What is culture?* To a business, team, organization, and families, culture is everything! As this book has laid out, thoughts lead to actions, actions lead to habits, and then habits lead to results. Most people believe that culture shows up in the results.

While this is true, I would argue that culture actually begins in the thoughts. Just take a look at a great company – this could be one you work for, work with, or at which you spend money. Perhaps you have seen their mission statements and mottos proudly hung on the wall.

Thoughts

Most businesses, teams, and organizations follow and live by those statements. However, we have all been around a business or organization that says all the right things about what their culture is, but yet this doesn't show up according to actions or words. The single most important reason for this is because they don't believe it. The commitment is not there, and they don't really believe the words they are saying. Many times, they actually incentivize the wrong behavior that becomes counterproductive to their culture, sometimes knowingly and other times unknowingly. But it all starts with thoughts.

Recently, our cable and internet went down and I called the customer service line. I pushed all the necessary buttons when prompted, and then listened as the recorded voice informed me the wait time was 15 minutes.

For the next 15+ minutes I listened to a blend of music and a recorded voice telling me how much they valued me as a customer, and that their number one goal is customer satisfaction.

Really? Were they trying to convince me, or themselves? While they may have the best intentions to live the culture mindset they speak of, the company's actions did not represent that same culture.

It is similarly demonstrated by a grocery store with 40 checkout lanes that never have more than three of them open at any given time.

What is the thinking behind that? What culture have they created for staff… and customers?

Southwest Airlines is one of the best examples of a company who

Thoughts

lives the values in which they promote. Here are the values taken from their website:

Live the Southwest Way – A Warrior's Spirit
- Work hard
- Desire to be the best
- Be courageous
- Display urgency
- Persevere
- Innovate

Servant's Heart
- Follow the Golden Rule
- Adhere to the principles
- Treat others with respect
- Put others first
- Be egalitarian
- Demonstrate proactive customer service
- Embrace the Southwest Airlines family

Fun-LUVing Attitude
- Have FUN
- Don't take yourself too seriously
- Maintain perspective
- Celebrate successes
- Enjoy your work
- Be a passionate team player

Work the Southwest Way
- Safety and reliability
- Friendly customer service
- Low cost

Thoughts

Think about the wording; a phraseology of these values is as unique as the thoughts themselves:

- A warrior spirit
- A servant's heart
- A fun-LUVing attitude

What does it mean to have a warrior spirit, and how does that show up? Southwest says that it means being fearless in terms of delivering the product. They want to be sensitive to the customers' space and schedules.

Treating others with respect is how they show up with a servant's heart. Notice it says *others*, not just customers. Put other people first, even the other employees. This is evident if you have taken a Southwest flight because you will clearly see the way the crew enjoys and values one another.

> Everything begins with your thoughts.

Lastly, there is a fun-LUVing (this is how Southwest spells it) attitude. They encourage their employees to have fun and to not take themselves too seriously. Over the last few years, I have seen several internet videos with crew members giving flight instructions in their own personal delivery style. One crew member delivered it in the form of a rap song, and another did so in cartoon character voices.

The best part of all of it is that the company recognizes and awards employees who exhibit these values. They are lauded in newsletters, on the website, and by video. The amazing statistic is the slim two percent voluntary turnover rate of employees, practically unheard of for most organizations. Southwest also receives tens of thousands of commendations a year. This is a real example of a company who believes and lives the values (the culture) it professes to hold.

Thoughts

This same idea of culture shows up in marriages and within families. It is the way I think, what I think, and how I think about my wife that later shows up in my actions. The way we think about our children is how we show up.

Are we putting our families, spouses, or loved ones on hold while they wait for us? Or do we think about them with a warrior spirit, act with a servant's heart, and create a fun-loving environment? Your culture is everything! Create one that you can be proud of – one that sets you above and apart from everyone else.

It all starts with our thoughts. Start with thinking bigger, creating a vision, and dreaming again. Put your plan together and get to work! It is time to… NOW MAKE GOOD!

Thoughts

Chapter 1 – Action Plan

- Describe and write the following:
    1. A clear vision statement powered by a strong "Why."
    2. Develop your 1-3-5 GPS Plan.
- List what steps you need to take to protect your thinking. (i.e. Limit time with certain people, no longer watch the news, etc.)
- What steps do you need to take to improve your thoughts? Who can help?
- Make a list of what books you should read, what podcasts you should listen to, or what seminars you should attend to open your thoughts to new ideas.

Thoughts

CHAPTER TWO

TAKING ACTION

TAKING ACTION

—PRODUCTIVITY

Taking action isn't about just working hard. It's about working smarter and harder.

Resources are often limited when it comes to the amount of focus, energy, and time in which work is possible. Therefore, the choices about how to apply yourself matter greatly. You can try to just work harder and push through. We have all done it. However, eventually you will suffer from one of the three diseases:

1. Burn-out!
2. Rust-out!
3. Blow-out!

Burn-out

Burn-out comes when you are not looking to improve your thinking, actions, habits, or results. For many, burn-out often shows up as a complete surprise because you just go through the routine of the day. If you are on "auto-pilot" each day, you may be suffering from the early on-set of burn-out!

Actions

Rust-out

Rust-out happens when you are taking action solely for

the sake of taking action. You are merely keeping yourself busy, but you are not getting anything meaningful accomplished. I see this often when people have been doing something for a long time and have stopped trying to learn or improve.

You must stay in a state of constant improvement! Even professionals practice and improve!

Blow-out

Blow-out is a product of several things. Mostly, it is allowing yourself to be part of someone else's plan and not your own plan. This feeling of being taken advantage of creeps in over time, and then…boom!

Burn-out, rust-out, or blow-out can be experienced in all areas of life: mental, physical, spiritual, financial, or relational. It is important that you improve your thinking to change course, otherwise, you will remain unproductive!

Action and Productivity Challenges

Have you ever felt like you are making some progress only to feel like you had to start over again? Yes, me too!

In my experience, the following three challenges are what have held me back from being productive and taking massive action:

1. Inability to say NO
2. Not having a clear plan
3. Fear

Actions

Inability to Say No

Herein lies one of the greatest challenges of any successful person: learning the ability to say NO when it interferes with what you have said YES to.

When you set a goal and make a commitment to a certain outcome, you need to continually resist those things that are attractive but distracting you from your goals. Saying NO is what helps keep you on track and in control. It is what allows you to be focused on your success versus those who try to do it all or try to please everybody.

This reminds me of a coaching client I had who struggled with saying "No" to his clients. He was a real estate agent and worked really hard to provide for his wife and child. Unfortunately, he did not create boundaries or protect his priorities.

He shared with me that he consistently made promises to attend his son's track meets and school functions, but would fail to attend when his clients came calling. One day his middle-school-aged son wrote him an email sharing how he respected his dad for how hard he worked, but felt hurt by the fact that he couldn't trust him when he said he was going to come to his events.

Ouch! How heartbreaking! By saying "Yes" to his clients, he was saying "No" to his son. By not placing boundaries, he allowed himself to become distracted and led away from his priorities.

My mentor and friend, Dave Jenks, says that all successful people need to be aware of the three distraction goblins of ADDICTION, DIVERSION, and DISTRACTION. If you say "Yes" to them, you can kiss your dreams goodbye.

Actions

 Once you have set your goals, made your plans, and announced your intentions, you will be tested. It will be difficult. You have to give up your ADDICTIONS: those habits of action or inaction that are not productive.

You have to ignore those DIVERSIONS that are attractive but don't lead to where you want to go. And, you have to shut out those DISTRACTIONS that interrupt you, disrupt you, and take you off track.

> Why is saying "no" so hard to do?

You must be willing to look honestly at your actions and habits and identify the things that divert or distract from your priorities. Remember, learning to say "No" will make you available to say "Yes" to those things that help you achieve results!

Not Having a Clear Plan

I have come to believe that successful use of time is the ability to use time wisely, and in a way that serves you best. It is so easy for people to get caught up in spending time responding to other people's crises or emergencies instead of following, adhering to, or implementing their own plans. If you do not stick to your own plan, then you will become a part of someone else's.

There is always enough time to do what it takes to move forward toward successful goals. However, the determining factor centers around who is in charge of that time. The answer must always be the same: YOU!

Think about how you start your day. It comes naturally to most of us to check email, text messages, or other forms of communication as we begin our day. We then let the messages set the tone for what we do and how we do it.

Actions

Email is one of the worst distractions. It is nothing

more than someone else sending me their priorities. If I let it, email can now make me part of someone else's plan and priorities. They make it sound urgent and important, yet the truth is they are almost never urgent or important for me.

I have specific times of the day in which I read and respond to emails. This allows me to be ready to focus and respond on my time. Additionally, I do not open and read the email unless I am ready to respond at that moment. This way I do not have to try and remember what to respond to later.

Admittedly, it is easy to let others drive your schedule. Examine your situation and crank up your assertiveness if you need to. Protect your time!

Fear

Is it possible that we fear what will bring us success? As strange as it sounds, many people do fear success, and fear can paralyze us from taking action if we don't get it under control.

Why do people let fear stop them from taking action? It is easier to stay comfortable with what I know and where I am then to change my situation. Or do I fear the pressure to perform at a new level of action? What happens if I fail? What will others think?

A question to always ask yourself when faced with fear regarding a course of action is, "What am I allowing to create this fear? And is it true or not?"

If I know the action is the right action to take, I do it regardless of fear. Through experience I have found my success is usually just on the other side of that fear.

Actions

Taking Massive Action

If you are going to take action, why not make it MASSIVE? If you are going to set a goal, why not make it MASSIVE? Is the goal exciting and massive enough to get you out of bed? Is the action massive enough to move you toward the direction you desire? Does it move you from taking average action to MASSIVE ACTION?

Just as I discussed before, it all starts with your thinking. Taking MASSIVE ACTION requires a different mindset. I have worked on training myself to not have average thoughts but instead to think big!

Sometimes those around you believe this level of thinking and action is unnecessary or even borderline insane. It goes beyond the typical social norms of what most people do. Many of those close to me challenge my actions, saying things like, "Why do you want to have a company that big?" or "When is enough, enough?"

> What are you allowing to create fear in your life … and is it true?

What does that even mean? The reason I want a bigger company is to employ more people and to make more money so that I can serve on a bigger platform. But they don't know my *why* and so for them it seems crazy.

Taking MASSIVE ACTION requires you to challenge your own predefined guidelines of being average. Average is safe. Average is comfortable. Average is acceptable.

Here are three myths of taking MASSIVE ACTION. Each myth is explained, and then followed by a short reflection on its truth.

Actions

MYTH 1 – *Fear of Going BIG:* Believe it or not, many people have a fear of taking massive action and going big. Why? There is a myth that going big is more complex. Many of the entrepreneurs I meet have really bought into this myth of going big with their business. *How will I manage it? Who will I hire? I have never had employees and it scares me. My business is good now and it will just be more complicated to grow big.*

TRUTH: Yes, your challenges and problems may seem bigger, but this is a sign of taking MASSIVE ACTION. To get MASSIVE RESULTS, you must have different challenges. When my business partner and I were challenged to take our regional company to a national organization, we immediately bought into this myth. How will we do it? We know all of our current customers, and we like that. After serious reflection, we realized these were stories we were telling ourselves. The truth was: *Why not us?* We didn't need to have it all figured out, but we knew that we needed to go big to accomplish our goals. The scariest and most exciting day was when we started to get customers whom we didn't know. It was scary because it felt like the business was growing beyond what we could hold on to, and yet it was exciting because the business was growing. Doubt and fear of losing control are the roots of this first myth.

Five years later, I can assure you that it is no more work being 10x larger as an organization. Any additional complexity is offset by the ability to hire more people. (*For specific instruction on how to attract, interview, and hire employees please refer to my previous book Five Plus One: The Entrepreneurs Formula For Success. – Discipline 5*).

Actions

MYTH 2 – *Waiting for Permission:* Too often I hear people comment about the sense of empowerment they feel after talking with a coach, therapist, or mentor.

They say things like, "I feel like they gave me permission to feel a certain way or to act a certain way." It is not surprising that we feel this way when we consider how most of us were raised. We needed to ask for permission to do just about anything.

Let me share a rather embarrassing moment to illustrate this example. I remember being in first grade and having to use the bathroom. I raised my hand to ask permission as we were required to do. The teacher continued to ignore me. I couldn't hold it much longer when she finally asked what I needed. I asked to use the bathroom and she told me to wait until lunch. Well, you can figure out how that story ended.

> **TRUTH:** The truth is that you don't need to wait for permission. Who are you waiting for to give you permission anyway? The problem is that while you wait for permission to take MASSIVE ACTION, you squander your most precious resource: YOUR TIME! No one will give you permission to take action necessary for the results you desire! The stars will never be aligned. You must get outside your comfort zone. You must jump!

> **MYTH 3 – *Fear of Making a Mistake or of Failure:* *What if I fail? What if I make a mistake?* These are the thoughts and self-talk we fill our heads with when we take MASSIVE ACTION. Those close to me already think that it's crazy to take such actions, and the last thing I want to do is prove them right.

> **TRUTH:** First, find me a successful person in any field and I will show you a list of mistakes and failures. The point is not that they made mistakes or had failures, but it's what they did after that. Howard Schultz, one of the founders of Starbucks, had to raise $1.6 million dollars in

Actions

the course of growing his idea from concept to reality. "In the course of one year I spent trying to raise money, I spoke to 242 people and 217 said 'No.'" What if Howard would have said, "This is a mistake," or "I have failed?" Today he is the CEO and has a worth of at least $3 billion. It wasn't an easy journey, yet it was one full of taking action. One of my mentors challenged me to run toward those things that I fear. The reason I fear doing certain things is more than likely because I know subconsciously I actually need to do them. For example, I fear any kind of public speaking. I knew that if I wanted to accomplish the MASSIVE goals I have made, then I would need to do many public speaking engagements. I continue to work with those who are really skilled in this area to help give me the confidence to be a great public speaker and overcome that fear.

What are you fearful of? What do you need to do? What do you need to do NOW? Don't wait. Take MASSIVE ACTION today! Don't put it off! It is time to... NOW MAKE GOOD!

Actions

Chapter 2: Action Steps

- What or who do you need to say "No" to so that you can be able to say "Yes" to what you need to?
- What fears are getting in the way of you living the life you desire? Once you list them, ask yourself, "Is that true?"
- What can you do to take MASSIVE ACTION today?

Actions

CHAPTER THREE

HABITS

HABITS

—WE ALL HAVE THEM

Our habits allow us to consistently perform at a higher level. We know that it takes time and discipline to develop such habits. Managing our time is part of it, but more importantly it's about developing the skills, systems, and standards that allow you to be the Master of Your Time.

The Framework of Timing

In Stephen Covey's best-selling book, *The Seven Habits of Highly Effective People*, the first three habits are about being productive and effective. Simply put, they are:

#1 – Be Proactive
"Be Proactive" means just that: be active. It is so easy to get distracted. For years, I had a postcard on my desk that said, "Is what I am doing now an income producing activity?" It was a simple reminder to make sure I was focused on being proactive.

#2 – Begin With the End in Mind
When you are clear about where you are going and what it looks like, then it is easier to decide what to do with your time. Once something is clear to you, then you can make it clear to others.

#3 – Do First Things First

Habits

When you step back to evaluate what is a top priority, and then find yourself following through, success will follow. This is a sign of your development of a keen sense of timing. The most successful people I know do the most important activity first. This way, nothing else has a chance of getting in the way.

Your Time, Your Way

I have come to believe that successful use of time is the ability to use time in your own way. If you don't have a plan for your time, then you'll be part of someone else's plan.

There is always enough time to do what is necessary to develop the habits that lead to success. That is why you must be in charge of your time! Admittedly, it is easy to let others drive your schedule. Examine your situation and assume control. Protect your time!

Master Skills for Your Time Control

Each of us will need to become a master of these five time-related elements:

1. **Goal Setting:** Going through the process of a 1-3-5 GPS will help you know what you want to accomplish. It is of course necessary to know where you want to go and what you want to accomplish. Setting the goal alone will not get you there, but it is the first step in the right direction.

2. **Action Planning:** There are certain steps or activities required to get you to where you want to go. You set the goal, and then take the necessary steps to accomplish this goal.

3. **Outcome Framing:** As discussed in Chapter One, you need a vision for what you want the

Habits

outcome to be. This applies to your goals and action steps as well as your daily routines. Do you know what you want the result to be before you start the activity?

4. **Calendaring to the Now:** Can you convert your goals and action steps to your calendar? Until they are on your calendar, then they are not real! If it is not on your calendar, then it doesn't exist.

5. **Time-Blocking for Priorities:** Take control of your time so that you get the things done that are most important and most effective. To do so requires you to block and protect this time.

Time-Blocking for Priorities

Priorities are necessary in order to create the habits that lead to success and impactful results. Time blocking is the technique of putting important activities on the calendar so that they are not put off or neglected. When you block the time needed to get things done, you will make sure they are accomplished.

In order to do this, you must own both the task and the time it takes to get it done. You are not a victim. You must take ownership of your own time on this earth to get things done. It helps to have adequate time for first things first.

The more you do this, the better you'll get at it. You will become a master at estimating how much time is required to develop the habits for achieving your goals. It means fewer disruptions and staying on task. In addition, others will respect your efforts. In this manner, your actions will match your intentions. There is power in that!

Habits

What should I time block?

Keeping in mind your available time, here are several things that I block off first:

- Time off with family for vacations
- Planning time to work on my business – not just in my business
- Generating leads for business
- Morning routine to set my day right

Building the correct habits is what we are after, and since only you set your goal, the responsibility is yours to block off your time in a way that works best for you. I use little reminders as well as my calendar to help me stay focused on my priorities. Provide yourself with reminders to help you stay focused on the habits you are creating.

Protect Your Priorities

Something I do to protect my priorities is to turn off my email notifications on all my devices. *Wait…what? Really? You can do that?* Those are the typical responses I get when I share this point. Yes, you can and you should!

You don't need to respond to email every single time your phone dings or vibrates notifying you of a new message. Not only is it a complete distraction, but it can actually take you away from your immediate priority.

A few years ago, I expressed interest in the product of a particular vendor. I really wanted to buy his product and believed that it would help us increase growth and retention within our organization. He was located out of state,

Habits

making it difficult to find time to connect and strike a deal. A few months later, I was asked to speak at a company in his area and to discuss topics from my book *Five Plus One, The Entrepreneur's Formula For Success*. I notified him that I would be there for the day and would have about 15 minutes between the end of my presentation and when I needed to leave for the airport.

> Are you letting others determine your priorities?

"Perfect timing," I said as we sat in the restaurant area of the hotel. "I only have 15 minutes, so let's get to business." He opened his tablet, propped it toward himself, and began to tell me more about his product. *Wow. Impressive*, I thought. He had notes on his tablet about me and how his product could help us. Then…

"Ding."

He looked at his tablet, swiped left and continued with his pitch. "Ding." Again, he swiped left and continued speaking. But after three or four more times of this repeating about every thirty seconds, I asked, "May I ask why your tablet keeps dinging?" His response floored me. "I am expecting a very important email regarding a huge deal, and I will need to respond immediately."

To which I responded, "Well, that is interesting because I was expecting a very important meeting and was hoping to purchase immediately."

Of course, I didn't purchase from him. I realized if I wasn't important enough for 15 minutes to get me as a client, then he certainly wouldn't have time for me when I was his client.

Habits

Stop letting someone else send you their priority. That's all email is. I promise, nothing in your email is an emergency. If your house was on fire while you were at work, would your neighbor email you? Someone would find a way to contact you and let you know.

I schedule time throughout my day to check email and get back to people. This one step has helped me protect the priorities that are right in front of me.

The 21-Day Myth

For most of my life, I have been told that habits are formed by completing a task every day for 21 days. Unfortunately, this is not so.

In an article in the *Huffington Post*, James Clear pointed out that the 21-day myth started from a misunderstood connection of Dr. Maxwell Maltz's work on self-image. Maltz was a plastic surgeon in the 1950s and noticed a pattern with his patients. He noticed that it took his patients about 21 days to get used to the new surgery. For example, he found that a patient who had an arm or leg amputated would experience phantom limb pain for about 21 days before they adjusted to the loss of the limb.

Dr. Maltz also noticed that he experienced similar behaviors in his own life regarding the habits formed over a 21-day period. So, in 1960 he published his thoughts on behavior in a book called *Psycho-Cybernetics*. The book was a best-seller with more than 30 million copies sold. Many motivational speakers, trainers, and personal development leaders have quoted Dr. Maltz for years. This myth has been spread and continues to be discussed as what it takes to develop a habit.

Habits

The 66-Day Truth

In 2009, Phillippa Lally, a health psychology researcher

at University College London, decided to lead a research team and study just how long it takes to form a habit. She published her findings in the *European Journal of Social Psychology*.

Lally researched the habits of 96 participants over a 12-week period. At the end of the 12 weeks, the team analyzed the data and determined that it takes 66 days for a new behavior to become automatic.

It is worth noting that there was a great deal of variation within each participant's results during the study. For example, it only took one person 18 days to reach peak automaticity, while another didn't get there at all by the end. Further, some behaviors became habitual more easily than others. Simple behaviors, such as drinking water, reached automaticity quickly, while others – like exercise – took longer.

> **What are the threats to your good habits?**

The research shows that it takes typically just over two months for most of our actions to really become a habit. How can this knowledge help? Think about the last time you made a New Year's Resolution to start exercising, eat healthier, to improve your relationship with your significant other, or to get a better job. You were certainly all excited and truly committed. You started your routines and were doing great, but then about three to four weeks into it you were already off track.

This has happened to me more times than I would like to admit. What happened? I quit too early! I didn't know that I needed to stay with it longer to develop that habit. Now, when I look at the actions that I want to develop into a habit, I look more long-term in my planning.

Habits

Threats to Your Habits:

#1 – Turbulence

Turbulence is bound to occur as you create these habits. As you get productive and begin to create habits of productivity, the obstacles come your way. Imagine that you have never flown in a plane. Just as you board, the pilot comes over the speakers and says, "We're taking off soon and expecting a pretty smooth flight. However, as soon as we take off, we will experience 5-10 minutes of rough air and bouncing, but then it should smooth out and be clear sailing." Then when that happens and you feel the bumps, because you anticipated the situation and expected the outcome, the warning most likely relieved your mind and saved you from unnecessary worry.

Now imagine the reverse. What if you boarded a plane for the first time in your life and no one warned you about the immediate turbulence you would experience? If all of a sudden, you started to bump and shake, the experience would understandably be unnerving and unsettling.

Obviously, no one would like to experience the second example. So what you must do is prepare yourself for what is to come on your own proverbial plane. The harder you push, the further you reach; the bigger your goals, the greater your actions; and the more solidified your habits, the bigger the turbulence that is coming your way.

You've got to know it's coming so you don't quit.

A little more than a year ago, I developed the great habit of going to the gym five nights a week, and the results were showing up! I was sleeping better and lost weight, and I felt great! The turbulence came for me one night in November 2015 as I went to play basketball with some new friends. It had been five years since the last time I'd

Habits

stepped onto a basketball court, due to a ruptured left Achilles tendon.

After recovering from that ordeal, I finally got back on the court but was a little rusty having not played for so long. On any account, I was enjoying the exercise.

Well, for about an hour that is, until I was chasing a loose ball and heard a shotgun go off! That's what it sounds like when you rupture your Achilles. Yes, you got it – I ruptured my right Achilles that night. I am not sure what the statistical odds are that you can rupture both in a lifetime, but as my surgeon explained, "100%."

I said, "Really?"

"For you it is 100%," he replied. "So it doesn't really matter what the odds actually are." Good point!

Within just a few weeks of not going to the gym and working out, I found myself tired and quickly winded. It was terribly depressing.

This injury was far worse than my previous rupture. It has since taken me nearly one full year to get to a point that I could even jog again. But once I got my thinking right and took the necessary actions (like blocking time to go the gym), it wasn't long before the habit was developed to once again be a regular attendee at the gym.

#2 – Boredom

For me, I know that I must do what others are not willing to do so that I can have what others are not willing to go after. In fact, part of it is that it really is so easy to do, and, therefore, it is easy not to do. That's the key – truth be told, that's what happens – these priorities and habits

Habits

are so easy to do that others on the outside looking in will say that it can't be that simple. One of the threats to your productivity is the fact that it can potentially become boring.

Some of those boring habits lead to the results for which you are looking because they are the income-producing priorities that have to be done.

One way to combat the threat of boredom is to ask, "How can I make it better?"

If going to the gym gets boring, then how can you make it better? If your relationship is boring, then how can you make it better?

Remember, you are in control! Don't wait to make it better. Do it now!

The Ceiling

As you develop and master the habits necessary to produce the results you are after, you will discover a new challenge of the ceiling. The ceiling is sometimes described as a "plateau." It is when you do everything you know how to do, but you are not getting any better results.

You really only have a couple of options once you hit this ceiling:

1. Continue to do what you've always done.
2. Pursue other opportunities.
3. Improve your thinking, actions, and habits!

Habits

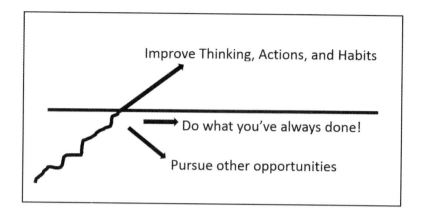

Continue to Do What You Have Always Done

This choice is the most common and the easiest because it requires that no effort or change takes place. It is also frustrating, however, because you continue to do the same things while expecting a different result. Some call this the definition of insanity!

If you are approaching each day complaining about the same job, same problems, and getting the same result, then you are stuck in option one. The good news is that you can change it. But it requires you to change your frame of thinking.

"But you don't understand, I can't get a new job. I have been here 20 years. Who would hire a 50-year-old when all the new hires in this industry are in their 20s?" You are right!

With that thinking, nobody would hire you. Change your thinking to positive, confident self-talk. Get into action and start looking for and talking to those who can help. Improve your skills and develop them to aid you in reaching that better place.

Habits

54

You can certainly stay at the ceiling, or you can change your thoughts, actions, habits and get a different result! Break through that ceiling to a higher level. But it is up to you.

Pursue Other Opportunities

Some people experience this mindset of constantly pursuing other opportunities as a way of escaping the reality of needing to improve and/or change their situations. This is evident when they are getting new jobs every six months. They are not satisfied with the current positions, managers, or businesses, and so it must be that they were meant for something else.

This is the problem – they chase the next job because the grass is always greener with the new opportunity.

Then guess what? A few months later…same story, different lawn.

> Whatever will make you and your situation better … do it now.

Others experience this by changing relationships every few months. They can't find the right person. "I will never find Mr. Right!" Even worse, are those who have been in committed relationships for some time and have hit the ceiling. Instead of improving their own thinking, actions, or habits they begin to pursue other options.

Imagine if instead of blaming your partner, you changed *your* thinking and improved *your* actions. You might just see a different result.

The unfortunate thing is that because your thinking never changes, then you find yourself hitting the ceiling again with the new options you pursue.
The question to ask is, "Am I pursuing another

Habits

opportunity to avoid or to improve?" If you don't improve your thinking, then it is really just a matter of time before the pattern repeats itself.

Improve Your Thinking, Actions, and Habits

No matter the industry, the undertaking, or the challenge, everyone will hit the ceiling at some point. In business, I experience this all the time. Knowing how to get through to the next level is the key! The only way to get through is to improve what and how I think. I then must get into action by improving my skills. Once I have defined my desired outcome and improved the corrected actions, I must practice them in such a way that they become a habit.

When you hit the ceiling, embrace it. Know that the thinking, actions, and habits you have developed to this point have gotten you to where you are. If you are to improve, then you must improve your thinking, actions, and habits. You will then achieve better results and new levels. Now, you will rush to hit the next ceiling because you know what is on the next floor: Success!

When you see success as your duty, then you approach your actions with a focused energy. I feel a moral obligation to those who are counting on me to be successful. When you set a goal that is focused on success, don't let anything get in the way!

Remember, you hired up for a tough guy... break through that ceiling... NOW MAKE GOOD!

Habits

56

Chapter 3: Action Steps

- Rate yourself on a scale of 1-10 (1 being unproductive and 10 being massively productive) on how well you use your time to accomplish your goals. What do you need to do to improve to the next higher number?
- What actions do you need to take to protect your priorities?
- What do you need to do to break through the current ceiling that is holding you back?

Habits

.

CHAPTER FOUR

RESULTS

RESULTS

—WE ALL WANT THEM

As you get your thoughts right, take MASSIVE ACTION, and are consistent in your habits, then you must be accountable for your results. Any of us could far exceed our goals or fall a little short of anticipated results, yet either way we need to be accountable for our results. This does not necessarily mean just being accountable to others – sometimes it also means that we are accountable for others.

Accountability

You can either have results or make excuses, but not both. You can either be a victim of circumstances, or you can be accountable for results. There is a lot of talk in the business world about accountability. Usually it is about how to hold others accountable, and it tends to have a disciplinary tone to it. "I'm going to hold them accountable," sounds a lot like "I'm going to call them on the carpet." Those who hold themselves accountable do so in a much different, more productive way.

Accountable people say, "If it is to be, it is up to me!" They don't play the victim game and they don't look for excuses. If they mess up, they 'fess up. They don't apologize; they take ownership and **Results** make it right. When good things happen, they take credit and feel good because they made it happen.

Success is *not* about what happens to you; it is about what you do to make it happen! Assume control of your own life and design your future. Don't wait for permission to make it happen.

The hard truth for each of us is that we are where we are in life entirely because of the decisions and actions we have made or not made.

Accountability is the way we improve performance, generate better results, and create personal satisfaction. Accountability is the key to ownership and to effective leadership.

> You
> need to
> own it.

Several years ago I was struggling from the recent failure of a business venture that left me devastated both personally and financially. As mentioned in a previous chapter, the best way to get out of turbulence is to get into activity, so I quickly launched my next business. I was just a few months into that new venture when I had an experience that challenged me to the core.

One day I was in the middle of a meeting with a group of potential clients when my phone rang. It was my wife calling. She knew we had important meetings that day, so I figured it had to be something important. I excused myself and took the call.

I said, "Hey sweetie, what's up?"

She said, "I am at the store trying to pay for groceries, but the card won't work."

I would like to say this was an isolated incident, but it was becoming a regular occurrence. "Let me check the bank account online and call you right back." I could feel the humiliation in her voice as she stood in line with food on the counter and other people waiting impatiently behind her.

Results

I called her back and said, "We have $27 in our account. Get whatever is necessary that is under $27." She said okay and hung up the phone. My heart sank and my stomach turned as everything within my being felt for my wife at that moment. I knew she was embarrassed, and I was humiliated. I felt like a failure.

Initially, I went into victim mode. I wanted to be upset at everything and everyone around me for any reason – anything to deflect the fact that I was in that spot because of the decisions I had made. To be truly accountable, I needed to own it! I needed to own the situation.

The truth is that each of us who find ourselves in a similar spot have to own the fact that we are in that situation because of the decisions we have made. The good news is that awareness and ownership is the first step toward moving from being a victim of the situation to being accountable for results.

From that moment on, I decided that I would do whatever was necessary to achieve success so that my wife would never have to go through that scenario again.

If things were going to get better, then it was up to me. I wasn't going to wait for anyone else!

I didn't need someone else to hold me accountable to improve. The truth is, none of us really hold another person accountable. The results are simply the results. Each of us have to own them.

At the root of the word *accountability* is the word "count" or "account." Accountability, therefore, means the ability to keep track of, count, or account for something. It means to measure what happens. That is truly what accountability is: a returning and reporting of my results to whomever I am accountable.

Results

When I work with others, I use the following questions when reporting results.

The 5 Questions of Accountability

1. What were you trying to accomplish? (What was the goal?)
2. How did you do? (Did you accomplish the goal?)
3. How do you feel about that? (Self-awareness and self-discovery.)
4. Based on what you learned, what will you do next? (What is your next goal?)
5. What, if anything, will get in your way? (Use foresight to predict your threats.)

If it takes you longer than 15 minutes to discuss these questions with someone, then you are not in accountability any longer – you are in therapy!

I work with many entrepreneurs and business leaders who hire me to help them reach their goals. We regularly visit the 5 *Questions of Accountability*. Often, I already know the goals they have set. However, even if I think I know, I still ask all the questions.

> Nobody really needs to be held accountable. They can do that themselves!

The accountability is in the returning and reporting of the results. For example, I recently followed up with one of my clients regarding a goal he had set. He wanted to add ten new clients to his business.

Results

I moved through the questions:

1. What were you trying to accomplish or what was your goal?

Answer: "My goal was ten new clients last month."

2. How did you do?

Answer: "I got four new clients."

3. How do you feel about having only achieved four new clients when the goal was ten?

Answer: His answer was a little surprising and told me a lot about his mindset. He responded, "Well, I am not happy that I didn't get ten, but I am not that disappointed. I worked really hard, but I think it's just the time of the year. Nobody really wants my service this time of year... so I am just not going to beat myself up over it."

4. What will you do next or what is your new goal?

Answer: "My goal for the next month is six new clients."

5. What, if anything, will get in the way of you getting six new clients and how do we avoid that so you can get hit your goal?

Answer: "Well, I am not sure. I mean I have never gotten more than five new clients, so six will be difficult this time of year. Maybe I should set a goal of four because then I know I **Results** can hit it for sure."

 I asked, "What would happen if you increased your

efforts by ten times rather than lowering your goal?" After a bit of discussion, he conceded that he was letting fear, negative thinking, and other obstacles distract him from his goal. I asked how he could change or improve his thinking to get a different result. We then made additional plans to achieve the new goal.

> Never lower the goal ... ever.

You may think that this process is too difficult, or that I should have just cut him some slack. But remember, this wasn't *my* goal! This was *his* goal and that goal was driven with a powerful *why*. As a coach, mentor, and friend, I am pushing him to what he told me he wanted to achieve.

Feedback

All great performers (athletes, singers, musicians, sales people) record their performances and then review their work. They do this to get feedback because they know it improves their results. That is why I say, "Feedback is the breakfast of champions!" Truly, champions use feedback to help them be more accountable for results.

Seek out people who will give you honest and direct feedback. Take to heart what they are telling you and how you can improve. Use feedback to help you make the necessary adjustments to achieve your goals and the desired results!

Interested in results or committed for results

As a business coach and mentor, I often talk with my clients about the difference between a prospect and a client. I hear entrepreneurs excitedly tell me about their new clients, and I ask if they have signed up or paid for the product or respective service. "Well, not yet, but they

Results

are interested." That's right! They are interested, but not yet committed. They are not yet clients. They are prospects until they are committed.

"There is a difference between interest and commitment. When you are interested in doing something, you do it only when it's convenient. When you are committed to something, you accept no excuses – only results," says author and management expert Ken Blanchard.

When you have not yet achieved the results for which you are looking, you either increase your excuses or efforts – but you can't do both. This is evident when a goal is set within a company or organization and it becomes clear by the midway point that the organization is not quite on track to hit the goal. A meeting is soon called and the entire discussion centers on lowering the goal. The mindset is that the goal was too unattainable to begin with, so the decision is made by all in the meeting to lower it to a more reasonable goal to keep morale high. At no point during the meeting is it discussed how they might increase their current effort toward the goal. The easiest choice is to lower the goal instead of focusing on an increase in effort. This is not the right approach. Never lower the goal! Increase your efforts!

As the leader of a national organization, I am often faced with this kind of situation. Should we adjust the goals? But when it comes right down to it, that is not within my thinking – I am just not wired that way. As I write this book, I am faced with a goal for next year that seems daunting to some yet exciting to others. Some have suggested we should lower the goal. Why? Why lower our destination?

Results

Instead, I gathered my team and we discussed how we might improve our incentives and recognition programs to encourage growth. At no point in our meeting did we ever discuss or mention lowering our goals. We have made announcements to our membership regarding the improvements, and it has energized their efforts. Imagine if I had instead announced that we were lowering our goal. How would that have energized the group?

Conventional thinking is that lowering the goal makes it more achievable, and therefore increases morale, focus, and commitment. In truth, the opposite is true. When you lower a goal, you act defeated and you jeopardize morale.

The Results Equation

Raise Expectation + Lower Toleration = New Destination

When considering an increase of the efforts toward a goal, it is vital to also discuss an increase of the participants' expectations toward that goal. One of the quickest ways to do that is to raise the expectations. Clearly, lowering the goals does not raise the expectations.

Many businesses have even adopted minimum expectations as the maximum amount of effort. This can be seen in the marketing efforts of a restaurant that promotes the freshness or quality of their food. Think about this for a moment … "We have great food!"

Well, shouldn't you?

That is already the expectation, but now you are making that your value. You must raise the standards. During high school, I participated in the high jump competition. Early on, I learned that the two posts that the bar sits upon are called the standards.

At every meet, participants approach the official judge and request the height at which they wish to start. After all the jumpers have jumped, the judge raises the

Results

standards and the bar. The standards are literally raised. As these standards are raised, the expectations for who can clear that height changes. Each time the standards are raised, fewer jumpers are around for the next height.

Each time we raise our personal or professional expectations and standards, fewer bad habits can hang around. At the same time we are increasing and raising the expectations, we must additionally lower the tolerations. When we do this, we change our destination.

> Raise the standard and the winners will rise to the challenge.

Let me give you a real-life example from my business. At Master Networks, we organize local business networking chapters. There is an expectation that each member will attend the weekly meetings. However, life happens and, on occasion, meetings are missed. The expectation is that no more than three meetings each quarter should be missed.

We often have chapter leaders who do not hold to that expectation. They tolerate the behavior of some people who do not show up on a regular basis. It quickly becomes a pattern.

Look, I get it. I did the same early on when we were building the organization. The argument plays out in your head that if you lower the tolerance, the members will quit – at least that is what I thought.

A few years ago, we had a chapter meeting and this behavior was very much present. There were nearly 20 official members of the chapter, yet there might have been anywhere from 8-12 who showed up each week. We were concerned that if we raised the expectation to weekly attendance and lowered what we tolerated, we would ultimately have fewer members.

That is actually what happened, but only for a few weeks. When we asked for the commitment of the group, a few things changed. We had three who were interested but not committed and they quit the chapter. Three or four of the others were committed to accepting the raised expectation and began to show up on a weekly basis.

Once the previous behavior was no longer tolerated, we found that we started to attract new members nearly every week. Consequently, we had now changed the destination of the chapter!

If you have not achieved the results you are looking for, then start to work at it today. Don't wait. You are not promised another day, week, month, or year on this planet. It is time to achieve your goals… it is time to NOW MAKE GOOD!

Results

Chapter 4: Action Steps

- In what areas of your life do you need accountability?
- Who can help you with accountability in each area?
- Who do you trust to give you feedback in the key areas of improvement you desire?
- What expectations of yourself or others need to be raised?
- What are you currently tolerating that you should not?

Results

CHAPTER FIVE

PERSONAL DEVELOPMENT

PERSONAL DEVELOPMENT

—DEVELOPING A SYSTEMATIC APPROACH

How do we approach each day? Do we look for ways to grow and improve? Or, do we wait for the perfect situation and conditions to make our move?

I believe the best course is to work each day toward improving just a little more than the day before. I live by the mantra, "Constant improvement is better than delayed perfection." As you achieve success and see progress in your results, you will need to have a systematic approach to your own personal development.

The Power of One Percent

Writer James Clear published a compelling article that has stuck with me. It focused on the great Pat Riley and the remarkable power of getting just one percent better. Riley was the coach of the Los Angeles Lakers basketball team in the mid-eighties. He had, by all accounts, a successful team in 1986. The team started off the 1985-86 NBA season with a 29-5 record. But despite their talent, the Lakers stumbled in the 1986 playoffs.

James Clear goes on to share that Coach Riley "was tired of hearing about how much talent his players had and about how much promise they held." In the summer of 1986, Riley created a plan to help his players live up to their potential. He revealed a new program called the Career Best Effort (CBE). Riley says, "When players first join the Lakers, we track their basketball statistics all the way back to high school. I call this taking their number."

James Clear references the book, *When the Game was Ours*, by author Jackie MacMullan. In her book she explains the calculation by saying, "The Lakers coach recorded data from basic categories on the stat sheet, applied a plus or a minus to each column, and then divided the total by minutes played. He calculated a rating for each player and asked them to improve their output by at least 1 percent over the course of the season. If they succeeded, it would be a CBE or Career Best Effort!"

Throughout the 1987 season, Coach Riley was constantly comparing each player's CBE to his past performances and those of other players around the league. Imagine how motivating it would be each week to walk into the locker room and see your name next to other league leaders. This allowed each of the team members to be constantly aware of choices, actions, habits, and results.

The Los Angeles Lakers began the program in October of 1986. Eight months later, they were NBA Champions. Pat Riley also led the Lakers to another title the following year, making them the first team to win back-to-back NBA Championships in 20 years.

Imagine what one percent improvement would do for you in the different areas of your life. What impact would this have financially, health-wise, or relationally? Who is the Pat Riley for you in each area of your life? Seek out those who can push you to be even just 1% better!

Who vs. What

The first and most common approach is to ask, "What can I do to improve?" While this is the most natural place to start, it may only allow for short-term improvements because it allows more opportunity to let yourself off the hook. My recommendation is to ask *Who* instead of *What* for improvement. Who can I add to my life? Who has been or is where I want to be?

Everything I have in my life that is of any significance has come through a relationship. My five children have come into my life because of my wife, who is definitely my "significant other."

One of the best ways to improve is to get a mentor or coach. If I remember back to that day as I was sitting across the desk from Hugh Gregson, I can only imagine what would have happened if he hadn't been direct with me. His response could have easily been something like, "Hey, I can see why you are frustrated, homesick, and upset. Why don't you tap out and go home?"

> Everything of significance is from a relationship.

I would not have received the growth I needed, not experienced the success I've had, and not made the relationships I've ended up developing. Instead, that day put me on a path that transformed my life forever. That kind of love and friendship from a true mentor in life can set up a path and a trajectory to where you need to go.

How can you choose the right mentor or coach? My advice is to first hire a qualified coach or mentor. Secondly, pay them what they are worth. Last, do what they say. If they are truly qualified, then do what they say. If truly qualified, pay them what they are worth.

Step #1 – Hire Quality

What makes this person qualified? When I've hired qualified mentors or coaches in my life, one main qualification has been that they are or have been where I want to be. Plenty of people will be willing to give you advice. Family and friends give you lots of advice – mostly unsolicited. Plenty of people will charge you money and say they are certified coaches. That is fine – they have spent time mastering their craft, but that doesn't necessarily make them qualified to be your mentor or coach. In my experience, the best and most qualified need to have *walked the walk* before they *talk the talk*. They have to be able to take you through the valley where they have been. That's the qualification in my mind for what makes a great mentor or coach.

One way I add value in my own experience of coaching and mentoring others is the fact that I currently run several companies. I practice what I teach every single day. I am not teaching a theory or just something I learned in a course – I am sharing my wins and losses from real-life experience. That is a tremendous benefit to those who are looking to grow a business.

Step #2 – Do what they say

When you reach out and engage a coach, do what they say. At times, they are going to tell you things you may not want to hear, such as, "You hired up for a tough guy, now make good."

One of the mentors in my life challenged me to be more productive going forward. When I walked into his office and laid out business plans for each of my companies, he asked, "What do you think about this? How do you feel when these businesses begin to gain a level of success that produces financial results? How are you going to feel about this?"

My response was, "Wow, this is incredible. I will be really happy." But by the look on his face, you would think I had said something repulsive.

He looked at me and said, "At what point did you think this was about you?"

I paused because I wasn't catching on quickly to his point. I said, "I don't know what you mean. Help me out here."

"Are your parents alive?"

"Yes."

"Are they healthy?"

"Yes, mostly they are in good health."

"Will they always be?"

"I don't know."

"Do you have kids?"

"Yes, five."

"Healthy?"

"Yeah."

"Will they want to go to college? Get married? Will they be in need? Have you and your wife been out to dinner and seen someone in need? Or have you ever learned about someone at your church with a need and wished you were in a better situation to help? Well, all *this* is a bigger platform for you to serve. This is not about you!"

That direct instruction from my mentor changed my mindset forever. It wasn't so much that I was being selfish or not thinking of others, but he was challenging me to be driven by an even more powerful *why*. I immediately began to approach everything with a different view. Assuming this mentor was qualified (which he was), why wouldn't I do what he said?

Step #3 – Pay them what they are worth

Most people don't spend money on personal growth and development, yet the most important asset in your life is *you*. We tend to spend the least amount of money on ourselves – in areas of personal, spiritual, and physical development.

Why? The answer is simply because it is not tangible. If I invest money, what is my ROI? What is the interest I earn? The hard part about personal development and growth, including physical growth, is that it takes a long time. Therefore, we don't do it. We spend more money on planning our vacations than on our personal development.

Presently, I invest more per month on personal development than I was making per month in the first ten years of my married life. I started small, but over time this investment has continued to pay big dividends.

Chapter 5: Action Steps

- Identify a qualified coach.
- Hire that coach!
- Do what they say!
- Pay them what they are worth.

CHAPTER SIX

LEADERSHIP

LEADERSHIP

—BE A PERSON OF INFLUENCE

Success breeds more success. When you start to get results, it will attract others to you. This will require you to lead. When you lead, you don't just improve…you change the game! One of the most recognized authorities on leadership, John Maxwell, describes leadership with one word: *Influence*. It's nothing more, and nothing less.

At one point in my career, I was asked to step out of a sales position to become the office manager. This typically happens when the organization wants to promote the top sales person. He or she is put in a managerial position which doesn't take advantage of the person's strengths. It's no wonder the sales person often fails in this new role.

That's exactly what happened to me. Sales and leadership or management have nothing to do with each other. My sales success didn't mean that I knew how to lead. As John Maxwell describes, I definitely had not learned how to have influence with others. Sometimes our success takes us to a level in which our leadership can't keep us.

My success had taken me to a level in which my leadership was not developed enough to sustain me. I knew how to sell, but I had no idea how to lead. It was this experience that drove me to invest in learning the ways that I could be the best leader possible.

As you improve your results, you will achieve a new level of success. However, you will be limited by the lid of your leadership.

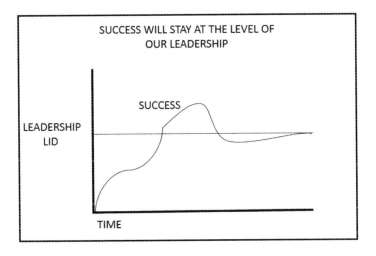

Assess yourself on a leadership scale from 1-10, with 1 being a level of leadership that would not compel anyone to follow you and a 10 being a leader of incredible influence.

Let's say you said you are a 7. Good for you! However, this means at best you will only attract another 7. Most likely you will attract 6s, 5s, and so on. If you are lucky enough to attract an 8, then you must raise your leadership level or your lid of 7 will cause them to find somewhere else, or someone else, to help them continue to grow.

Each of us must improve and raise that leadership lid before we are compelled by others who demand that lid be raised. If you said you were a 7, then the question to ask is, "What improvements should I make that can get me to an 8?" Don't try to jump to a 10. Work through each level in a systematic way. In leadership, there is no shortcut to the top!

PC3 – The Makeup of a Leader

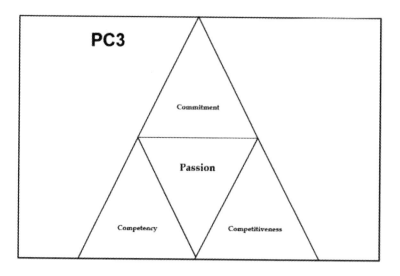

#1 – Passion

The word *passion* is often misunderstood, misused, and misrepresented. I hear it used when someone wants to quit something – they hit the ceiling of achievement. They often respond, "I'm just not passionate about it anymore." Yet the truth is that they just are not passionate about themselves or their life, and so nothing they do is passionate. It's a great excuse, a popular buzzword to respond in such a way.

Think about some of the greatest leaders you know. They typically have tremendous passion for what they do and who they serve. Take the example of great sports coaches. They have a passion for the game, for the success of the team, and for success. This shows up in everything they do!

Yes, I believe you should do what you love. But even when you love what you do and have passion for it, you still will come across challenges and struggles. It is at that point when many say they have lost their passion instead of digging into that passion to give them the strength to overcome the challenges.

#2 – Competency
Leaders are aware that they must constantly work to gain knowledge in every area of their lives. Yes, leaders are smart but not just book smart. They know what they should know and don't pretend to know something when they don't.

Athletic coaches at the highest levels must be competent beyond just the game, the x's and o's, the offense, and the defense. They also have to be competent about how to navigate the relationships with their players and other coaches. Competency is also a highly-valued concept within your industry and sphere of influence. Study and be a student of the game… the game of people!

I believe that especially over the next decade, those who are competent in the skill of connecting with people will be the next group of successful leaders – and our next group of millionaires.

#3 – Commitment
Commitment begins with your thoughts: the way you think and what you think. When you have the right type of thinking, then your belief shows up as commitment. You have heard the saying, "Actions speak louder than words." Commitment to the game, to others, and to the process at all levels will show up as commitment by way of actions. Imagine the commitment it takes to run a highly successful championship team. You must study films and playbooks, cultivating a dedication to practice. Honoring a commitment, even when you don't feel like it or when nobody is looking, is true dedication to commitment.

Think of the most influential leaders you know. Would you say that they are committed to their cause? Committed to those they lead? Of course, they are!

"Can I count on you for that?" This is one of my favorite questions to ask someone who has made a commitment to me. By asking this question, it tells me if they really are committed to the result. If I have to ask someone that question more than a few times, I know they can't be counted on.

#4 – Competitiveness

Leaders at the highest level are known to be competitive. This applies not only to themselves but also to those whom they lead. Leaders are not necessarily more competitive than those they serve. They are not trying to outdo or one-up those they lead. They bring out the competitiveness and success within others. Leaders must focus on building others up rather than drawing attention to themselves. Great leaders will give credit to the entire team for its success while also pushing the team to do more and reach higher.

PC-3 (Passion, Competency, Commitment, Competitiveness) is the formula for strong influential leadership. You must gain influence on and with others. As Seth Godin says in his book *Tribes*, "A tribe without a leader is just a crowd." Gaining influence is how you build your tribe, whether that tribe is your family, friends, or colleagues.

How are you leading?

Permission vs. Position

History books are full of leaders who exercised power based entirely on a perspective of the position they hold. This kind of leadership does not garner the influence necessary to achieve the goal because it forces others to follow. The positional leader who does not gain the permission to lead by those who follow... well, it typically doesn't end well.

In his book *21 Irrefutable Laws of Leadership*, John Maxwell shares the following story:

> During the final seconds of an especially tense game, Boston Celtics coach K.C. Jones called a time-out. As he gathered the players together at courtside, he diagrammed a play, only to have [Larry] Bird say, "Get the ball out to me and get everyone out of my way."
>
> Jones responded, "I'm the coach, and I will call the plays!" Then he turned to the other players and said, "Get the ball to Larry and get out of his way." It just shows that when the real leader speaks, people listen.

The goal is to move from being not just a leader of position, but to being a leader of permission. As leaders, if we want to truly have influence and engage those who follow, we must earn that influence.

Participating is not leading

People want to follow leaders who know where they are going. Even if those leaders aren't sure at that moment where they are going, they need to lead. Just merely participating is not the same as leading. Confidence matters.

I often see this demonstrated in our society as we watch our kids in sports. For many parents, every sport or activity seems to become a matter of winning participation trophies. That is all fine and good, but what are we rewarding? Yes, in sports there are winners and losers. That is a truth. In business, there are winners and losers. That is also a truth. If you are applying to college, there are some who will get in and others who won't – winners and losers. Applying for a job… again, there are winners and losers.

In my organizations, I reward those who participate, but make particular effort to award and recognize those who lead. People will work hard for money, but will die for want of recognition. My goal is to incentivize the desired behavior. Imagine if that's what we did with our kids in sports. How would they show up differently?

This world needs more people who reach beyond the mere act of participating, and step into leading. People want to follow individuals who have passion and direction. Are you just participating, or are you leading?

Effective Leadership: Transfer the Vision

One of my good friends and mentors, Logan Stout, shares his winning formula of effective leadership: a process he lives each day.

Every great leader has a vision, which is a clear idea for what is possible and how to achieve it. The challenge for most leaders occurs within the framework of two scenarios.

1. The vision is in their heads, and that's where it stays.
2. They tell everyone their vision and cannot get others to buy-in to the vision.

The best leaders have learned the skill of communication. They have learned how to create a clear vision, and they are capable of transferring that vision to others so that they can get buy-in from the team. Imagine a great football coach who says his goal is to win a division title but not the championship. Or the business manager who says, "My goal is to get 100 sales this month. Let's do it, team!" The problem is that is their goal and may not be the goal of everyone else. The team can't see the vision.

The most effective leaders have discovered how to take that vision and share the reasons and ways it will benefit the whole group. They say things like, "We have had a great year! We have improved our sales, which have provided more opportunities for each of us. Can you imagine what kinds of opportunities would be possible if we doubled or tripled our sales?" The team has to see what is possible for them, not just for you.

Great coaches ask, "What is it going to be like when we win the championship?" They inspire their teams by creating an image of the big goal as if it has already been fulfilled. Doing so gives the team freedom to picture and imagine what the achievement of their goal would feel like. This is an example of transferring the vision to the team – it's not just the coach's vision, but now the vision becomes the team's vision and they own it.

Effective Leadership: Transfer the belief

Throughout my life I have been very skilled at transferring my vision to others. A while ago, one of my mentors offered me some valuable feedback. He said that although I can easily help others see the vision, they may get overwhelmed when they think about how to accomplish it. Once I became aware of this weak point, I immediately began to implement a new approach to transferring the belief to the team. This one improvement helped me become a more effective leader.

Consider a coach who says something like this to his team: "Guys, you were the most prepared, you were the hungriest, and you worked the hardest this preseason. I have coached other teams and I can tell you that none of the other teams have been as prepared as this team is today. I know that you are prepared to win. I believe you have all you need to be successful today!"

Leaders understand they have to transfer the belief to those they lead. It's important not to draw attention to self, but instead to build up others. This is the task of a good leader. The best leaders don't just light a fire *under* someone, they light the fire *in* someone! It is remarkable what happens when people believe in their own ability to actually accomplish the vision.

Recently, I facilitated a private workshop for 12 entrepreneurs who were looking to improve their businesses. One young man came to the four-day workshop dressed in jeans and a t-shirt, and he was long overdue for a haircut.

> How exactly
> are you
> leading?

I spent the next four days helping him cast a vision that was big and bold. He saw what was possible. More importantly, after we laid out the plan and steps, he believed that he could accomplish the goal by taking MASSIVE ACTION!

In the days that passed, several people sent messages to me sharing how different he looked. He had a nice haircut, was dressed up, and seemed excited about the future.

Just a few months after that training, his business exploded! He began carrying himself differently. Others noticed it as well. Not only does he now believe in himself, but those around him are starting to believe in him, too. This has resulted in an immediate increase in referrals for his business. It's amazing what happens when people begin to believe in themselves. If you don't believe in yourself, then why would anyone else?

If you are struggling to get those around you to follow, then you may want to consider whether you have been able to effectively transfer the belief that the team has the ability to accomplish the goal. Bring them together and build the belief!

Train and Teach

A couple of years ago, I was asked to speak at an event of about 100 business leaders. I was looking forward to the event and being able to add value to the attendees. I was particularly excited because I had personally mentored the event host.

Just before I was to go on stage to present, a different leader got up to announce me. She had my biography in hand, but didn't refer to it. In the process, she made several incorrect statements regarding my qualifications.

As any polished speaker and leader would do, I ignored the improper introduction and continued with my presentation. When the event was over, the host came up to me. I asked, "How did I do?"

He responded, "Great!"

"Anything I could improve?"

He said, "Not that I can think of."

I always try and connect before I ever correct. This is an important step.

As a learning-based leader, he in turn asked, "Any feedback for me?"

I said, "Just one thing. I am curious why you had the other person on your team get up and make the introduction at the last minute."

He went on to explain that he saw this as an opportunity to empower that person as a leader in front of the other team members. On the surface, it seems like a great idea. However, he had neglected the important step of training and teaching the other person. His heart was in the right place, but he went straight to empowering her to do a job for which she was not effectively prepared. You must teach and train those you lead first before you empower them with the responsibility.

In my experience, the best leaders, organizations, and teams focus on training and teaching. They are learning-based and spend time on practicing to improve skills. They become masters of their craft.

Equip them with the tools

I often see what I call *Ignorance on Fire*. This happens when someone who has definitely seen the vision and has a ton of belief that they can accomplish the goal is not given the proper tools to be successful. In my experience, these people are the ones who burn-out, rust-out, or blow-out the fastest.

As the leader, you must make sure you give your people the necessary tools to accomplish the goal. I can teach all day long how to hit a golf ball, but if I never give you a club and a ball, then you will never actually hit the ball. Being equipped with the tools and training to accomplish the goal is crucial.

What are the tools you need to effectively lead others? Do those you lead have the necessary tools to accomplish their goals? If not, where can they acquire them? When you lead others, you must give them every resource they need to succeed.

Empower them

Nothing is more frustrating than to be given a job only to have a leader take it back. I have to remind myself and our team: "One of the great things about your job is it's your job!"

I was the assistant coach for a high school football team for a few years. It was an amazing and awesome experience to work with so many great, young men. We worked toward a common goal and believed we could achieve it.

At halftime of one particular away game, I recall that we were getting our tails kicked. We were playing the previous year's state champions, and they were a tough team! It was 42-6 at the half. The entire team was defeated.

> Winning at the end depends on what you do right now.

As the team gathered at the end of the field for instructions and motivation, the head coach turned to me in frustration and said, "Go get them fired up! I am too upset to tell them anything!" I turned to walk to the end of the field, thinking about what I might say to them. Should we give up? Should we quit? Or should we follow through on what we set out to accomplish? I knew they needed a transfer of belief!

I walked up and said, "Alright guys... you have two choices: quit or play the best football possible and let the score tell the story at the end. You committed to playing your best, and I believe that your best football is still yet to be played. You have put in the work and know what you need to do. It's time to make good!" The kids began responding, and I could feel the mood changing. I saw them looking at each other as if to say, "Yes, let's do this!"

Before I could say anything else, the head coach came up behind me and said, "That's not going to happen. We don't stand a chance playing like this. Just go out and finish without embarrassing us anymore." Then, he turned and walked away.

I was stunned... and pissed! Truthfully, I am not sure if the kids could have pulled off a comeback or not, but it didn't matter. I believed in them, and at that moment, I lost respect and trust for the coach. He had empowered me at that moment to do a job, but then he turned around and completely undermined me. Even worse, he did it in front of the team. Fortunately, I had a good relationship with the other coaches and the team, and so it did not affect my leadership or influence with them.

This story is a real-life example of how it can cripple your team if you empower them to do a job only to take it back from them. Someone trusts you... so trust them!

Support them

The last step in the *Winning Formula of Effective Leadership* is to support the team. This means that at all times you must support them, even when – and probably especially when – they make a mistake. Nothing is more disheartening than bringing a problem to the attention of a leader and them blaming a team member. Mistakes are part of being human. But a good leader sees those mistakes as learning opportunities.

Remember, leadership is influence. One of the best ways to build that influence is through trust. Trust develops over time as you support your team.

Chapter 6: Action Steps

- What are you doing to improve your own personal development?
- List the qualities of the leaders you admire. Develop and implement a plan to work on each characteristic you admire in other leaders.
- Identify an opportunity to lead a group of people. (Church group, networking group, or charity)

CHAPTER SEVEN

NOW MAKE GOOD

NOW MAKE GOOD

—IT IS YOUR TURN

It is time to *Now Make Good* in all areas of our lives. Don't wait! The time is now!

I invite you to join me on a journey of constant improvement in the five areas of each of our lives.

Mental

It all starts here. What are we feeding our brains? Garbage in, then garbage out. Most of the things that challenge us really are a function of our thinking. Do we look at each as a problem, or as an opportunity? Knowing that each challenge may present the ability for new opportunities to win is an exciting proposition.

This starts with training our ability to think differently. Read good books, listen to inspiring leaders, and eliminate the negative voices around us and within us.

A few years ago, my wife and I stopped watching the news because we recognized how negative every story seemed. We realized that we did not feel any better afterward. We were not inspired nor mentally stimulated in any way by watching the news.

What will you do to increase your mental capacity and improve your thinking? How will you protect your thinking? Who will you add in your life to help challenge your thinking?

Whatever it is that you want to accomplish, you can do it! You were built for greatness! If not you, then who? If not now, then when?

You've got this… Now Make Good!

Physical

This body you have is the only one you get. It may not be perfect, but it's yours!

In some ways it is like a vehicle. You need to take care of it, keep it clean, fill it with fuel, and maintain it. However, unlike that vehicle, when parts of your body start to fail, there may not be replacement parts.

This is probably one of the areas in my life that I need to focus on the most. I have been very casual in the past when it comes to my physical health. In fact, at the start of writing this book, I deliberately set out to improve this area of my life.

It started first with my thinking. It hasn't changed overnight, but over time it is improving. I have begun to look at food differently. Instead of thinking in terms of taste, I look at food as fuel – and the truth is that it can be both. I work hard each day to protect my thought process concerning the relationship between food and working out.

I created my 1-3-5 GPS and put it into action. I also pre-plan and cook my meals each Sunday, and I even hired a coach to assist me with my meal plan and exercise routine. If you are reading this right now and thinking, "I can't afford a coach," or "I don't know a personal trainer," or whatever excuse you may have – stop it! Protect your thinking!

I exercise five to six times a week and have asked for the support of those around me to help me create these activities to help me form productive habits.

I have not yet achieved my desired result, but I believe that will happen shortly. I am excited about the progress I see and how much better I feel.

> Take that first step, no matter how small it might feel to you.

Wherever you are, there you are. I mean, if you need to start then just start. Take the first step! You can do it! You owe it to those who need you to be in better health. NOW MAKE GOOD!

If you have made this a top priority and are mastering your physical health, well… congratulations! I know the amount of work that goes into such a task. My challenge to you is to help those around you. So many people need the belief that they can achieve results, and you can be their support!

Spiritual

Regardless of your religious beliefs, it is important to get clear about what drives you. If you believe in God, in a higher power, or something else, then it is important to gain clarity concerning your beliefs. A strong spiritual foundation brings tremendous balance in life.

Each day, it's important to take time to read, study, ponder, meditate, or pray. This time is a powerful period to clear your mind and allow for attracting instruction. My study, meditation, and prayer time is a protected time for me each day. I look forward to this time to clear my mind and get connected to what is important. I find that as I study, ponder, and pray, I open myself up to instructions from God. When I receive this instruction, then I know that it is time to Now Make Good!

Financial

I haven't met very many people who feel like they have mastered this area of their life. In fact, even those I know who have done well in this area want to continue to improve. The fact is, that is true for all areas.

If you are not where you want to be financially, then I would challenge you to change it! Change your thinking. Think in abundance and not in scarcity. Think about how you can improve your situation. Who can you learn from? What could you read and study that could help you learn the skills to improve your financial situation?

Recently, I met with a business person who was struggling with cash flow. After reviewing her financials, I asked what she thought she could do to improve. She responded, "Well, I think if we cut this expense and maybe let this person go, then we should be in the black each month."

"Yes, you may need to cut some expenses, but I think you are running pretty lean," I replied. "The problem is not an expense problem. What you really have is an income problem."

The fact that she could actually do something to improve her income had never occurred to her. In her mind this was an expense issue. So if she could do both – cut expenses and increase income – she could dramatically improve cash flow quickly.

Is that the same for us in our personal lives? In our early married years, the only financial discussion my wife and I had was what we could cut. After we cut all we could, it still seemed that our financial situation didn't improve. I realized that we had only focused on one part of the equation. From that moment we started to discuss how to increase income as well.

Money is good for the good it can do. Money is the great revealer. Money reveals the corrupt as well as the caring. It will reveal who we are. It is time to build a legacy for those who are counting on us to help. Remember, it is not about you, but it is about those you can help and serve. It is time to improve your financial situation. You can do it! It is time to NOW MAKE GOOD!

Relational

I left this area last for a reason. Each of the previous areas of life could all improve by developing relationships. Think about it… you want to improve your mental, physical, spiritual, and financial areas in life? Then improve the relationships in those areas!

Are there current relationships that need to improve? Yes! All of them. Just like the other areas, they take work, effort, and committed time.

Tell those you care about that you love them… often. Show them through your actions that you care. Take care and protect the current relationships you have. While each of us needs to improve the current relationships, we also need to foster new encouraging relationships in our lives.

You are the average of your five closest relationships. Maybe you have heard a similar statement at some point. This is what I have heard for many years and thought it was a cute meme that people posted on Facebook or Instagram. However, over the last three years I have come to see this statement as a true depiction of my life.

I have been strategic, specific, and purposeful about whom I want to have a relationship with. Yes, I like people. But, not all of these people can be in my inner life circle.

Some of my closest friends and mentors have only come into my life within the last couple of years. I can assure you that it didn't happen by accident. It was on purpose! I reached out to many people whom I looked up to with the intent of getting to know them. Not all of them were open to it, but several were. Now I call them friends and go through life with them.

It is time to improve the current relationships and make them great! It is time to seek out people who make you better – they demand it! It is time for each of us to be better spouses, better friends, and better partners. It is time to NOW MAKE GOOD!

Speed of implementation

A few months ago, I was asked to be on a small panel of business owners where the audience was able to ask questions of each of the panelists. One member of the audience asked us, "If you could name one key to your success, what would it be?" Trying to come up with just one is tough, but I answered, "The Speed of Implementation!" This is the ability to implement or act on what you have learned and to do so quickly.

I imagine you have had a few thoughts about how and what you want to improve as you read this book. The key is going to be how quickly you implement what you have learned. Don't wait! Act Now! Be Bold! You've hired up for a tough guy... NOW MAKE GOOD!

ACKNOWLEDGMENTS

I want to thank those who helped shape me to the man I am today. I am grateful to Hugh Gregson who inspired this book. Your leadership and tough love at an impressionable age is invaluable.

I want to thank my grandfathers, Dick Balsiger and Dean Wilson for always being an example of loving leadership, dedication to family, and incredible integrity. True tough guys!

I want to thank my wife, Jaclyn, for her love, support, and friendship. Thank you for always believing in me!

This book as a legacy for my five children: Ryan, McKenzie, Breydan, Jack, and Tate. I love you all!

Thank you to my parents Kent and Lynn Wilson for your belief, love, and support. I am grateful to my siblings: Jason, Kristin, and Katelyn for your support and love.

Terry and Jody for your faith and support of my dreams!

To my friend and mentor Dave Jenks, you are an incredible teacher!

NEXT STEPS

WILSON LEADERSHIP

Wilson Leadership is the delivery method in which we help business leaders and entrepreneurs implement the steps learned in the pages on this book.

I travel the country teaching and training the Five Plus One formula, and I am always being asked, "What now?" "How do I make this happen?" Wilson Leadership is the solution and answer to that question.

Visit my site to request a complementary coaching call at:
www.ChasWilson.com

NEXT LEVEL SUITE

We have made arrangements for our readers to get a special discount by entering the promo code "book" during checkout.

Next Level Suite is a simple to use and cost effective solution for a business to manage contacts. I use this system daily to communicate with my clients and prospects.

To learn more about Next Level Suite, visit:
www.nlsuite.com

MASTER NETWORKS

We are a membership network of learning-based, service-oriented entrepreneurs and business leaders. We meet in local chapters, powered by national and regional platforms, to connect, share, and prosper.

On a weekly basis, members have a full hour to focus on themselves and their businesses. They have the opportunity to teach others about their business via one minute sound bites and ten minute showcase presentations. The business training and personal development topics presented each week push them to work *on* their business, not just *in* their business. The referrals received from fellow chapter members help their businesses grow and their return on investment is realized.

Members can also step into leadership positions to have a direct impact on the excitement, growth, and energy of their chapters. Contribution and involvement of members leads to an even greater sense of connection to their Master Networks Chapters.

To learn more about Master Networks or to find a chapter near you, visit:

www.MasterNetworks.com